A TRUE BOOK™

Ancient China

MEL FRIEDMAN

Children's Press®
An Imprint of Scholastic Inc.
New York   Toronto   London   Auckland   Sydney
Mexico City   New Delhi   Hong Kong
Danbury, Connecticut

Content Consultant

Michael Lestz

Director of the O'Neill Asia Cum Laude Endowment, Trinity College

Professor of Chinese History

Library of Congress Cataloging-in-Publication Data

Friedman, Mel, 1946-
  Ancient China / by Mel Friedman.
    p. cm.—(True book series : ancient civilizations)
  Includes bibliographical references and index.
  ISBN-13: 978-0-531-25225-3 (lib. bdg.)   978-0-531-24106-6 (pbk.)
  ISBN-10: 0-531-25225-6 (lib. bdg.)   0-531-24106-8 (pbk.)

1. China—Civilization—to 221 B.C.—Juvenile literature. 2. China—Civilization—221 B.C.
to 960 A.D.—Juvenile literature. 3. China—Civilization—960-1644—Juvenile literature.
4. China—Antiquities—Juvenile literature. I. Title. II. Series.

DS741.65.F75 2010
951—dc22   2008051267

1 2 3 4 5 6 7 8 9 10 R 19 18 17 16 15 14 13 12 11 10

Find the Truth!

Everything you are about to read is true *except* for one of the sentences on this page.

Which one is **TRUE**?

T or F Chinese Checkers was invented in Germany.

T or F The Great Wall of China kept outsiders from entering China.

Find the answers in this book.

Chinese Checkers

Contents

THE BIG TRUTH!

Clay soldier from Qin
Shi Huangdi's tomb

Tomb Warriors

Who guards the tomb of China's
first emperor? 22

This Chinese mask is more than 3,000 years old.

A Chinese emperor
of the Tang dynasty

CHAPTER 1

Central Kingdom

The Chinese word for "China" is Zhongguo (JONG-gwaw). It means "Central Kingdom." For many centuries, China had the world's most advanced **civilization** (si-ve-li-ZAY-shen). China is the oldest civilization that still exists today.

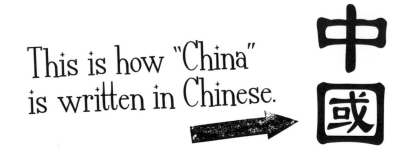

This is how "China" is written in Chinese. 中國

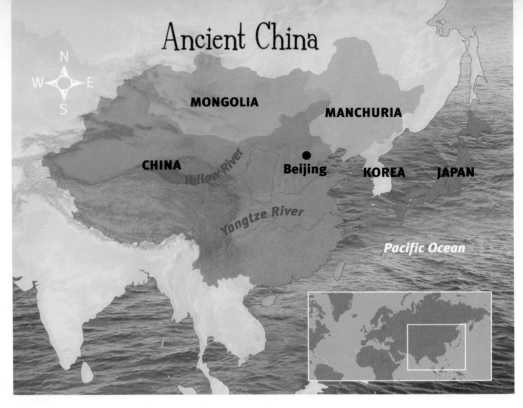

Ancient China

China grew larger as its borders were changed by war and trade.

Ties With the Past

The Chinese people have the longest continuously recorded history in the world. Four thousand years ago, the **ancestors** (AN-ses-ters) of today's Chinese lived in the Huang He (HWANG-he), or Yellow River Valley of north China. The culture and **traditions** they started there are still alive and well today.

Dominoes, tea, and inventions such as the wheelbarrow and the compass are just a few of the gifts that China has given to the world. The ancient Chinese also created some of the most remarkable works of art and architecture, including the Great Wall.

The Great Wall is about 4,000 miles (6,400 kilometers) long. →

It took millions of Chinese many centuries to build the Great Wall. The size of the Wall has changed over time.

Huangdi (HWAHNG-dee)

CHAPTER 2

Heroes and History

The Chinese people trace their history back to about 2800 B.C.E. According to stories and folktales from this time, China's first rulers were wise leaders. It's believed that these leaders invented many wonderful things and taught their people new skills.

Huangdi was called the Yellow Emperor. He is said to be the father of Chinese medicine and martial arts.

From Myth to Fact

One of these rulers, described in ancient Chinese stories, was Fu Xi (FOO-shee). He is often pictured as being half-man and half-snake. Fu Xi is said to have invented writing, fishing, and hunting. Another ruler, Yu (YEW) the Great, was known for building ditches and dams along the Yellow River to protect his people from floods. The Chinese consider him the founder of the Xia (SHYAH) **Dynasty** (DI-ne-stee) (about 2200–1766 B.C.E.), which may have been China's first state.

To the Chinese, Yu the Great is a symbol of hard work.

This mask is made of bronze.

It's not certain that these stories were based on fact. The Chinese began recording their history with the Shang (SHAHNG) Dynasty, which conquered the Xia in 1766 B.C.E. The Shang oversaw a set of states with five different capitals. Its people were mostly farmers in the Yellow River Valley. During the Shang Dynasty, people made bronze tools and containers. They also created beautiful objects made of white and green **jade**.

This cow is made of jade.

13

The dead were often buried with objects that would be useful to them in the afterlife. This Shang Dynasty grave included a chariot.

Of Kings and Gods

The Shang Dynasty had different levels of **society**. At the top was the king, followed by the priests and warriors. At the bottom were slaves. When a king died, many slaves and prisoners were often killed and buried with him to serve him in the **afterlife**. The Shang believed that their king could communicate with the gods. They also worshipped the spirits of their ancestors, a practice that is still important to some Chinese people today.

In about 1040 B.C.E., the Zhou (JOE) Dynasty rose to power, and the use of iron tools and weapons, which were much stronger than those made with bronze, spread gradually throughout China. Farmers now had better tools to grow and harvest more food. And so the Zhou rulers encouraged their people to move into new areas to farm. As a result, the size of the kingdom grew, and the Zhou people sometimes had to fight with neighboring kingdoms.

In Shang times, only warriors could use bronze weapons. Ordinary people had weapons made of stone.

Tang Shuyu was a prince during the Zhou Dynasty. The Jinci (GIN-tse) temple in northern China was built to honor him.

CHAPTER 3

The Golden Age of Thought

The Zhou Dynasty lasted almost 900 years—longer than any other dynasty in Chinese history! During this time, the area over which the Zhou kings actually ruled changed many times. The states within the Zhou Dynasty were ruled by kings, but all of the people worshipped a god called Tian (TYENN), or "Heaven."

Zhou "spade" coin

During the Zhou Dynasty, the Chinese began using coins as money.

A Close Watch on Rulers

The Zhou believed that if a ruler was kind and fair, Heaven would smile upon him and his people. If a ruler was evil or dishonest, Heaven would end his reign. The Chinese people saw floods and wars as possible signs that a ruler had lost Heaven's trust. In such times, the people felt they had a right to rebel against their ruler. This belief led to the collapse of many dynasties throughout Chinese history.

The dragon is a traditional symbol of the Chinese emperor.

The Zhou period was marked by many wars with tribes along the northern border of their kingdom. The Chinese wanted to find a way to make things more peaceful. By about the third century B.C.E., three different ideas were

Zhou warriors wore bronze armor. Most warriors went into battle in horse-drawn carts, called chariots.

being discussed. They were the teachings of Confucianism (cunh-FYOO-shun-ezem), Legalism, and Taoism (DOW-i-zem).

Top Teacher

Confucius was born into a poor family in northeast China in 551 B.C.E. As a young man, he studied ancient Chinese writings and was interested in tales of wise and caring rulers. Confucius wondered if good rulers could be found in his time. Later in life, Confucius became a teacher. He began wandering from kingdom to kingdom in search of leaders who might welcome his ideas for bringing peace to China by working together. Although he was not successful in his search, his ideas caught on among the people. Confucius died in 479 B.C.E., at the age of 72. Nearly four centuries later, Confucianism became China's official philosophy (fih-LOSS-uh-fee).

The ancient Chinese believed that life and nature were always changing. This idea is represented in the Yin-Yang symbol.

The Three Schools

With Confucianism, people were taught that society was like a family. Children had to obey parents. Wives had to obey husbands, and everyone had to obey the ruler. In return, all people, including the ruler, had to treat each other with respect.

Thinkers who believed in Legalism felt that harsh laws and punishments could keep people from doing evil things. The Qin (CHIN) Dynasty, used legalism to strengthen its army and conquer Chinese warring states. Believers in Taoism taught that people could achieve inner peace by living simple lives and accepting and working with what happened around them.

Tomb Warriors

For more than 2,000 years, an underground army of clay soldiers has watched over the tomb of China's first emperor, Qin Shi Huangdi (CHIN SHER HUANG-dee). Not long after he became emperor, Huangdi ordered some 700,000 workers to start building his burial tomb. His tomb was about as tall as the Statue of Liberty and almost as long as three football fields.

Life-Size Army

An army of 8,000 life-size clay soldiers, horses, and chariots stood in front of the tomb. The average soldier is 5.9 feet (1.8 meters) high.

These sculptures of military officials were created during the Tang Dynasty. They were buried in tombs.

CHAPTER 4

The Creative Spirit

Some of history's most important inventions—paper, printing, gunpowder, and the compass, originated in China. Other Chinese inventions include paper money, martial arts, fireworks, the folding umbrella, and even toilet paper! The ancient Chinese were also masters of the arts, including painting, sculpture, **calligraphy** (ke-LI-gre-fee), and architecture.

Figures were buried with the dead to keep them company.

First Compass

As early as 100 B.C.E., the Chinese discovered that a type of magnetic rock known as lodestone could be used to help them find north and south. They carved the rock into the shape of a spoon and placed it on a smooth brass plate that had markings indicating north, south, east, and west. The spoon would spin and when it stopped, the "handle" always pointed south. This was the first compass. Much later, between 850 and 1050 C.E., the Chinese developed the first needle compass for ocean travel. Between 1405 and 1433, the great Chinese explorer Zheng He (Jung-HUH) used the compass to make seven historic sea voyages. Zheng sailed a total distance of about 311,000 mi. (500,000 km).

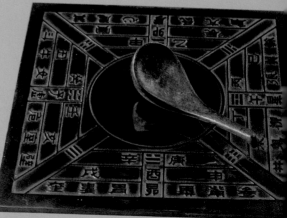

It is believed that the oldest piece of paper in the world dates back to the Han Dynasty.

Art Treasures

The development of paper and methods of printing made it possible for writing and art to spread across China and the rest of the world. Han (HAHN) Dynasty (206 B.C.E.–220 C.E.) artists became the first ever to paint on paper. During the Tang Dynasty (618–907 C.E.), which was a time of great Chinese poetry and calligraphy, book publishing grew. Experts believe that ancient Chinese authors wrote some of the world's first novels.

Performing Arts

Among the earliest Chinese musical instruments were flutes, bells, and drums. Later on, string, reed, and piped instruments were added. One of the oldest Chinese performing arts is storytelling. Through poetry, song, and shadow puppetry, the Chinese shared stories. Many storytellers performed for the wealthy rulers.

Shadow puppet

Ancient China Timeline

3000 B.C.E.
Chinese civilization begins.

1050 B.C.E.
Rise of the Zhou dynasty

28

Buildings

The ancient Chinese had a traditional way of building. Most buildings faced south—to catch the sun and good luck. Many had curved

The Forbidden City is an example of the traditional style of Chinese buildings.

roofs, which were believed to guard against evil spirits. Roof tiles came in many colors, but only the royal palace could have tiles of yellow, the royal color.

221 B.C.E.
Construction of the Great Wall of China begins.

618–907 C.E.
Chinese literature and art enters its golden age under the Tang Dynasty.

CHAPTER 5

Everyday Life

In ancient China, wealthy landowners could afford to have large families and grand homes. However, most Chinese were poor farmers. They usually had small families and simple homes. A father's word was law in all Chinese families. He decided whether a child should go to school, what job that child should take, and whom his child would marry.

In China, a person's family name comes before his or her first name.

Practice Makes Perfect!

From the beginning of the Zhou dynasty and onward, schools and learning were valued. In 124 B.C.E., the Han emperor started China's first university to select talented men to serve in government. The Han government paid the students' expenses as they attended school.

Before they invented paper, the Chinese wrote in up-and-down lines on strips of bamboo. The strips were tied together with string to make books.

Students read the writings of Confucius and studied math. Their teachers gave them exams to find the best leaders. Exam questions were written on bamboo strips. The students who did well on their exams went on to become Chinese leaders.

Boys and Girls

Chinese couples traditionally prayed for sons, not for daughters. Girls were not seen as equal to boys. Daughters of rich families were sometimes educated at home. Most girls were expected to learn only how to sew, cook, and care for a family. Girls from farm families also learned how to work in the fields alongside men.

Small feet were considered one mark of a woman's beauty and this led to a painful practice. For about 1,000 years, young girls, mostly from wealthy families, had their feet wrapped in bandages to keep their bones from growing.

Women with bound feet could hardly walk. The practice was banned in 1911.

Bride

Groom

A traditional Chinese wedding during the Manchu dynasty

Marriage for love was unheard of in ancient China. Some parents arranged future marriages for children who were as young as six. Many brides and grooms never met each other until their wedding day.

Games

Many of the toys and games that people still enjoy today came from ancient China. The jump rope, kites, the top, and Dominoes date back to this time. The Chinese invented two different types of chess. One is like the familiar game known throughout the world. The other is like the modern board game Othello. Chinese Checkers was not invented in China. It actually came from Germany!

Chinese chess often draws crowds when played on the street today.

36

According to Chinese folk beliefs, bad spirits can only move in a straight line. So paths are often zigzagged.

Magic and Ghosts

To the ancient Chinese, the world was alive with magic and ghosts. This explains how fireworks became an important part of Chinese New Year's celebrations. Fireworks were believed to scare away evil spirits from the old year. The ancient Chinese often decorated objects with images of tigers. Tigers were thought to keep away demons as well.

Warriors from Mongolia began attacking China in the 1200s.

CHAPTER 6

Strangers at the Gates

Throughout history, people from outside of China have tried to invade the country's borders.

The Great Wall was built to prevent these people, whom the Chinese considered **"barbarians,"** from entering China from the north and west regions of the country. But not even the Great Wall could keep them out. To better guard the borders, the Han emperor sent troops and settlers to the northwest in about 100 B.C.E.

The Mongol empire was the biggest in history.

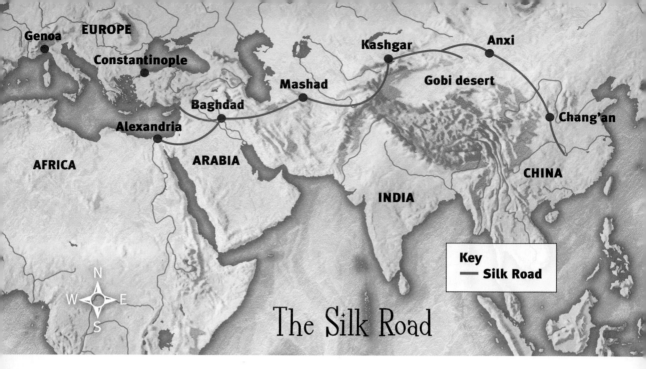

The Silk Road

Beyond the Borders

Soon the Han emperor received reports of strange, new countries beyond China's borders. He also learned that trading of Chinese goods was taking place along a string of camel routes now known as the Silk Road. Demand for beautiful Chinese silks was coming from far beyond China's borders. People outside China thought that silk was more valuable than gold.

People from other parts of Asia conquered regions of China many times in Chinese history. Two of these invaders, the Mongols and the Manchus, formed dynasties and expanded China's territories.

In the 1500s, people from Europe began arriving in China. They were interested in trading and spreading religion. But the Chinese people felt they needed little that these outsiders had to offer.

Manchu emperor

End of an Era

Along with European trade came change and internal troubles for China. Slowly, European governments had more influence over China. The Chinese blamed their Manchu rulers for this downfall and overthrew the last emperor in 1912.

Today, China is a modern, growing country. But the traditions and contributions of the past still live on and will continue to affect China, and the rest of the world, for many years to come. ★

Henry Pu Yi was the last emperor of China.

True Statistics

Average size of the largest section of the Great Wall: 25 ft. (7.6 m) high and 30 ft. (9 m) thick

Length of China's Yangtze River: 3,900 mi. (6,300 km), the longest river in Asia

Number of women emperors: 1, Wu Zetian (ZE-tee-en) of the Tang dynasty

Number of silkworms needed to produce one pound of silk: More than 2,000

Number of years it took to build the Forbidden City: 14

Luckiest number for the Chinese: 8 (because it sounds like the Chinese word for "good fortune")

Unluckiest number for the Chinese: 4 (because it sounds like Chinese word for "death")

Did you find the truth?

(T) Chinese Checkers was invented in Germany.

(F) The Great Wall of China kept outsiders from entering China.

Resources

Books

Brownlie, Alison. *China* (Destination Detectives). Chicago, ILL: Raintree, 2006.

Cotterell, Arthur. *Ancient China* (Eyewitness). New York: DK Pub., 2005.

Dramer, Kim. *People's Republic of China* (Enchantment of the World). New York: Children's Press, 2007.

Fontes, Justine, and Ron Fontes. *China* (A to Z). New York: Children's Press, 2003.

Marx, Trish. *Elephants and Golden Thrones: Inside China's Forbidden City.* New York: Abrams Books for Young Readers, 2008.

Morley, Jacqueline. *You Wouldn't Want to Work on the Great Wall of China!* New York: Franklin Watts, 2006.

O'Connor, Jane. *The Emperor's Silent Army: Terracotta Warriors of Ancient China.* New York: Viking, 2002.

Waterlow, Julia. *China.* North Mankato, MN: Cherrytree Books, 2005.

Zelenyj, Alexander. *Marco Polo: Overland to China* (In the Footsteps of Explorers). New York: Crabtree Publishing, 2006.

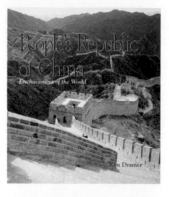

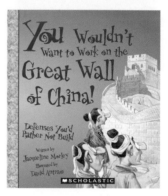

Organizations and Web Sites

Ancient Chinese Inventions

http://afe.easia.columbia.edu/song/readings/inventions_
timeline.htm
Discover a timeline of Chinese inventions.

Get a Chinese Name!

www.mandarintools.com/chinesename.html
Type in your English name and get your own Chinese name.
You also get to find out your sign in the Chinese zodiac!

Silk Road Foundation

www.silkroadfoundation.org
Find out everything you ever wanted to know about one
of the most famous trade routes in history.

The Palace Museum

4 Jingshan Qianjie 100009
Beijing, China
www.dpm.org.cn
See the art and architecture
of the Forbidden City.

Asian Art Museum

200 Larkin Street
San Francisco, CA 94102
(415) 581 3500
www.asianart.org
View artwork from the Asian
continent, including Chinese
porcelain, jade, and calligraphy.

Important Words

afterlife – life after death

ancestors (AN-ses-ters) – people from whom an individual
is descended

barbarians – a group of people considered rude
or uncivilized by another group of people

calligraphy (ke-LI-gre-fee) – the art of beautiful handwriting
done with a brush or pen

civilization (si-ve-li-ZAY-shen) – the way of life of a people

dynasty (DI-ne-stee) – a series of rulers from the same family

jade – a semiprecious stone usually with a deep green color

philosophy (fih-LOSS-uh-fee) – the study of truth, wisdom,
and the nature of reality

society – the members of a committee or group considered
together

traditions – information or beliefs handed down from
parents to children over many years

Index

Page numbers in **bold** indicate illustrations

About the Author

Mel Friedman is an award-winning journalist and children's book author. He has four graduate degrees from Columbia University, including one in East Asian studies. He also holds a B.A. in History from Lafayette College. Friedman has written or co-written more than two dozen children's books, both fiction and nonfiction. He speaks and reads Chinese, and spent a year in China teaching English at Beijing Normal University's branch campus in Zhuhai, Guangdong Province.